HOW TO HANDLE
BULLYING
Copyright © 2023 Samuel John Books

Did you know that around one in every four children experiences some kind of bullying at school?

That's a lot of children!

So, you must know how to spot bullying and how to deal with different bullying situations.

That's where this helpful anti-bullying guide comes in! Let's get started!

You see someone hitting your friend in the arm over and over again. Your friend asks him to stop, but he refuses. What do you do?
SCHOOL

If you see physical bullying, you should find the nearest teacher or parent to ask for help.

Never use physical violence just because someone else is doing it. Bullies need to learn that violence is not the answer.

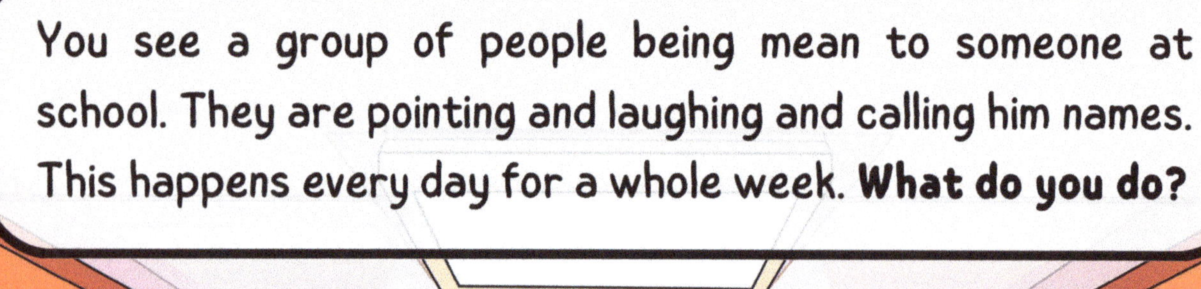

You see a group of people being mean to someone at school. They are pointing and laughing and calling him names. This happens every day for a whole week. **What do you do?**

Be brave and stick up for people you see being bullied. It is nice for them to know that they have people on their side to support them. Then, you should report the bullying to a teacher or responsible adult to get it to stop once and for all.

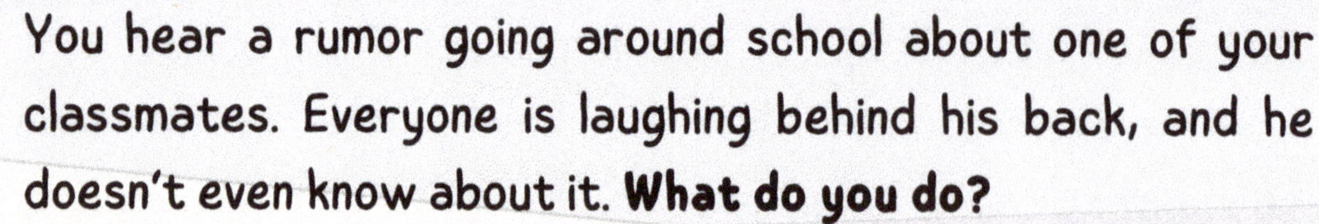
You hear a rumor going around school about one of your classmates. Everyone is laughing behind his back, and he doesn't even know about it. What do you do?

Tell your classmate about the rumor so he knows what is going on. When you hear the rumor being spread around school, tell people that it is not pleasant to spread rumors. Never spread the rumor yourself. You should offer to go to the principal with your classmate to explain what is going on.

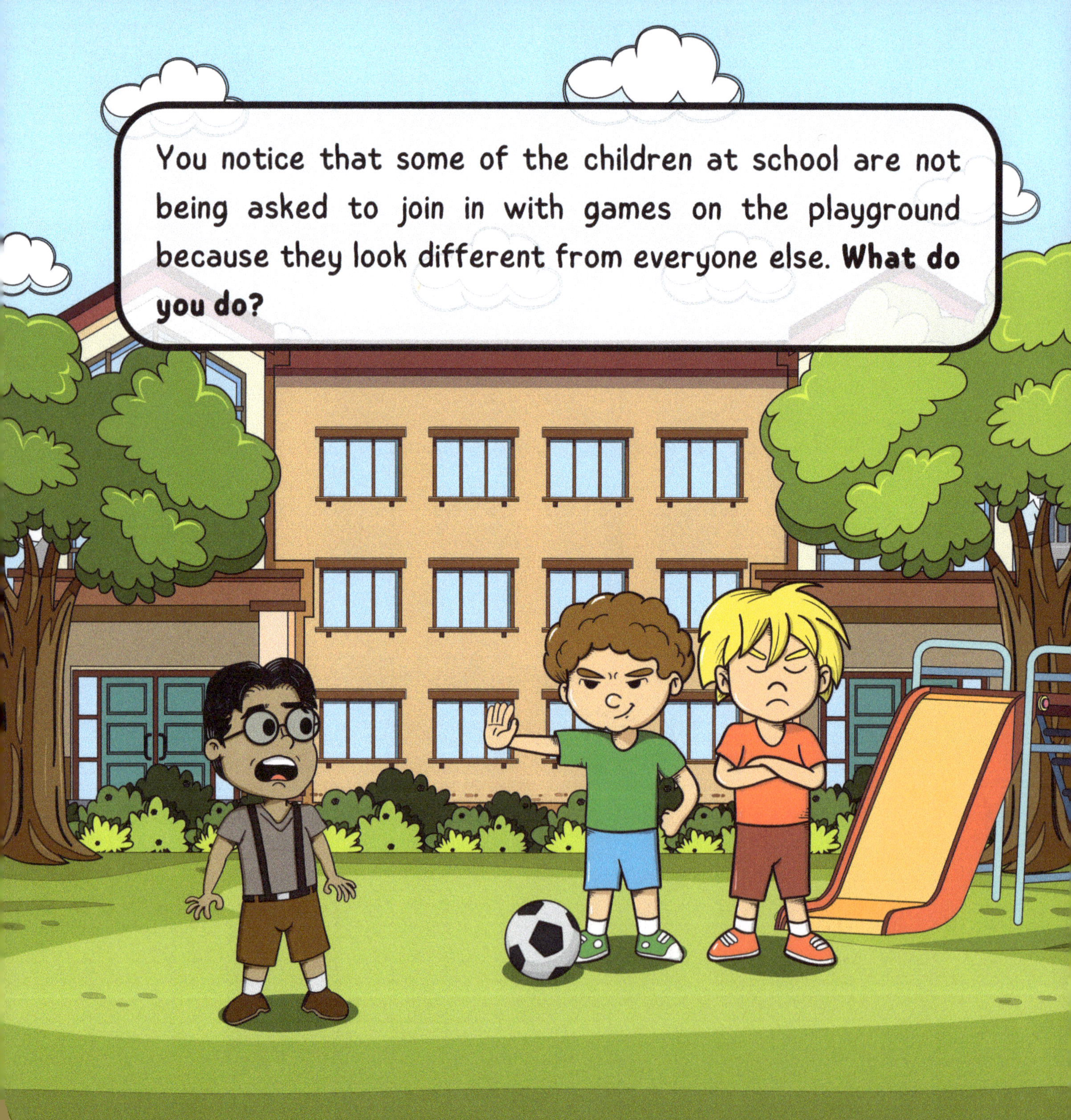
You notice that some of the children at school are not being asked to join in with games on the playground because they look different from everyone else. **What do you do?**

You should never treat people differently because of the color of their skin, how they look, how they sound, or where they come from. You should explain this to your friends and suggest that you include everyone in the game. If they refuse, it would be kind to go and start a new game with the children who have been left out. Then tell a teacher what is happening.

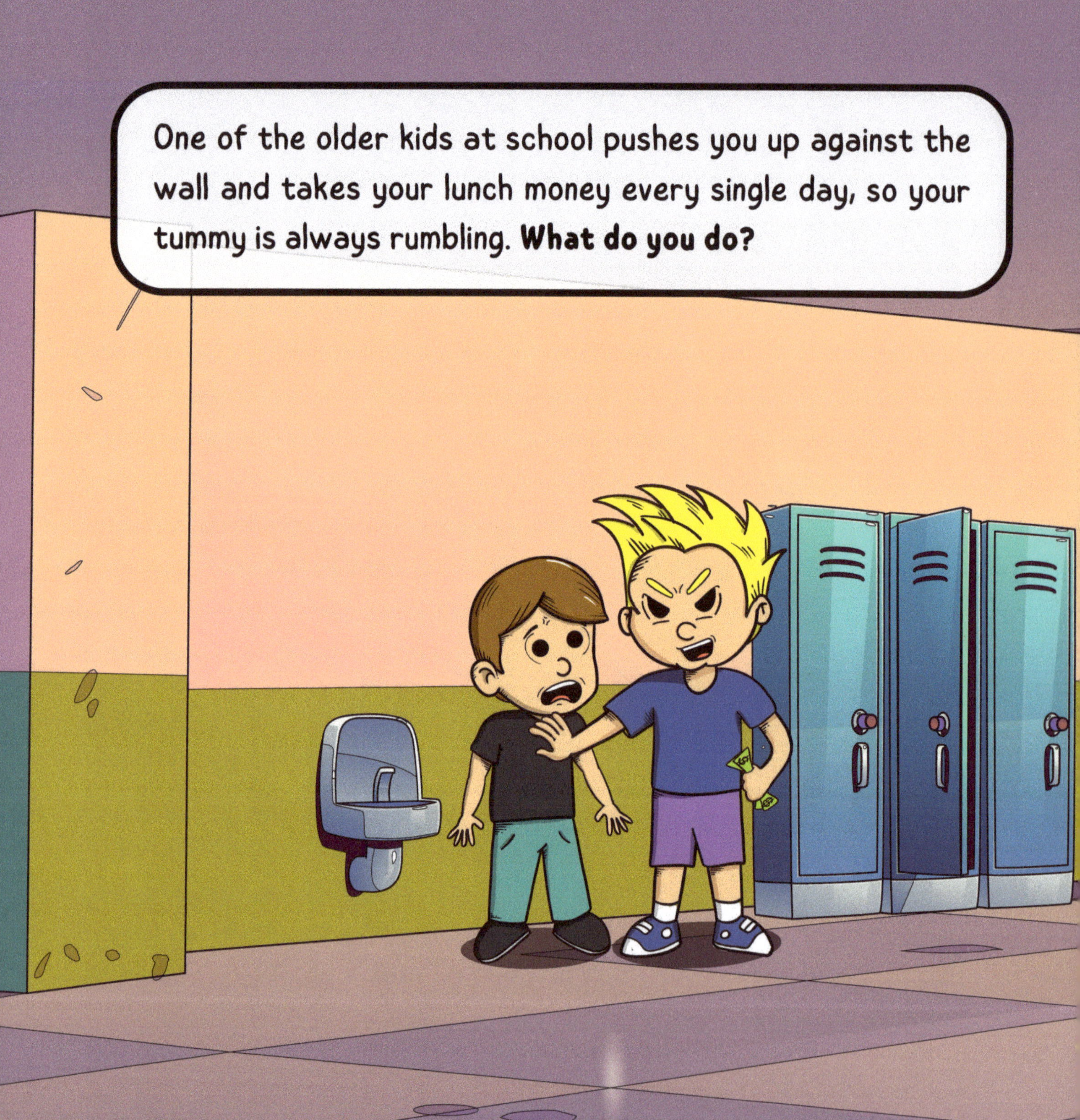

One of the older kids at school pushes you up against the wall and takes your lunch money every single day, so your tummy is always rumbling. **What do you do?**

Even though it seems scary, the best thing to do is tell your parents, family, or teacher about what is happening. The only way to stop bullying is to talk about it. Adults can talk to the bully and make sure they leave you alone in the future.

You and your friends are joking around and having fun. You joke about your friend's pencil case, and he gets upset. They tell you that sometimes you make too many mean jokes, which upsets them. **What do you do?**

Sometimes, you can bully someone without even knowing you are doing it. Something may not seem like bullying to you, but it feels like bullying to someone else. If your friend tells you that you are being a bully, do not get angry and defensive. Say you are sorry and try hard to stop doing whatever it is that upsets them.

You love wearing bright and colorful clothes to school, but some of the other children make fun of you when you do. What do you do?
203

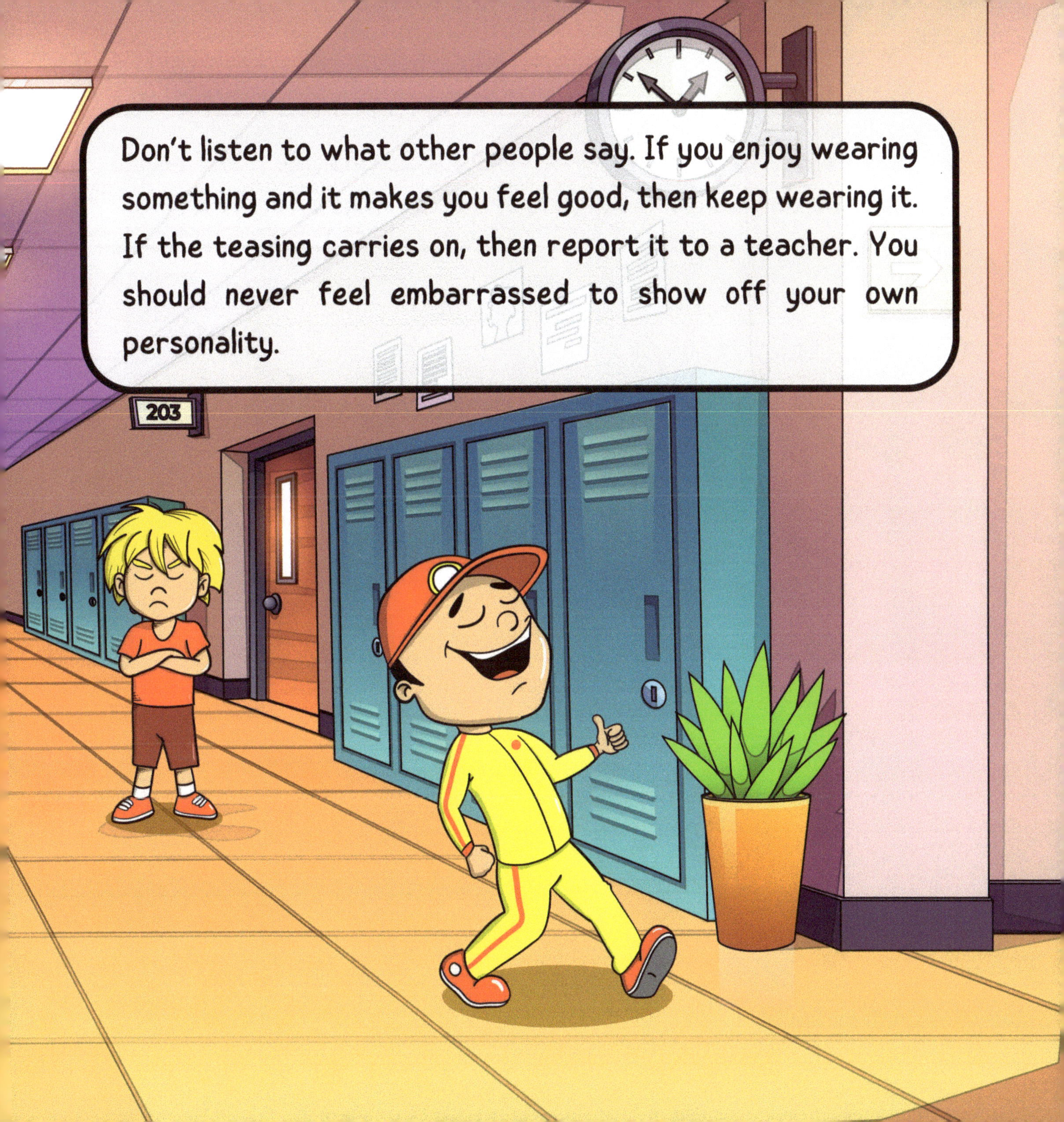

Don't listen to what other people say. If you enjoy wearing something and it makes you feel good, then keep wearing it. If the teasing carries on, then report it to a teacher. You should never feel embarrassed to show off your own personality.
203

You regularly receive texts telling you that you are a loser, but you don't know who they are from. **What do you do?**

Ask whoever it is to stop, then block the number. If you keep getting texts or messages online, you should talk to your parents, family members, or a teacher about the bullying. Online bullying is just as serious as bullying in person.

How to tell when someone is being a bully:

- They are using physical violence
- They are making fun of people
- They are starting mean rumors
- They are leaving people out on purpose
- They are making other people feel sad on purpose
- They get other people to join in with their bullying
- They make you feel small and helpless

What to do when you see a bully:

- Let the victim know that you are there to help
- Give them a hug if the victim seems upset
- Offer to go with them to tell a teacher
- Tell a teacher or adult on their behalf if they are too scared
- Never join in with bullying
- Tell a bully that what they are doing is wrong

You should never be afraid to report a bully. It can seem scary to stand up to a bully, but it is the only way to make the bullying stop.

If you are the victim of bullying or witness someone else being bullied, then you should report it to a teacher or responsible adult as soon as possible. Bullying is wrong and you shouldn't have to go through it.

I want to ask you a favor so that this book reaches more people, and that is that you rate it with a sincere opinion on the platform where you purchased it.

With that small gesture, you will be helping me to carry on with new projects.

I can't wait to start creating my next book for you!

You can leave your review directly here. It will only take you a few seconds.

www.bit.ly/bullyingreview

Thank you in advance for taking time to share your experience. I appreciate your support!

See you soon!

LEARN WITH OUR EDUCATIONAL CHILDREN'S BOOKS

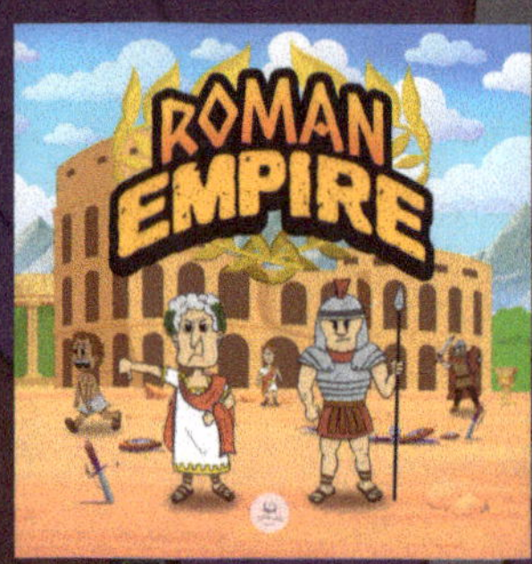

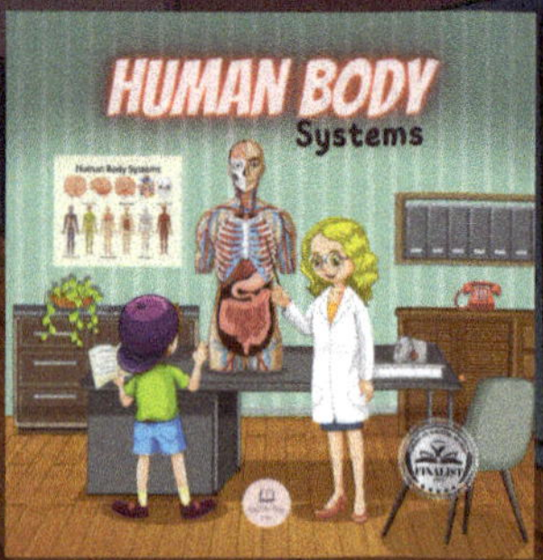

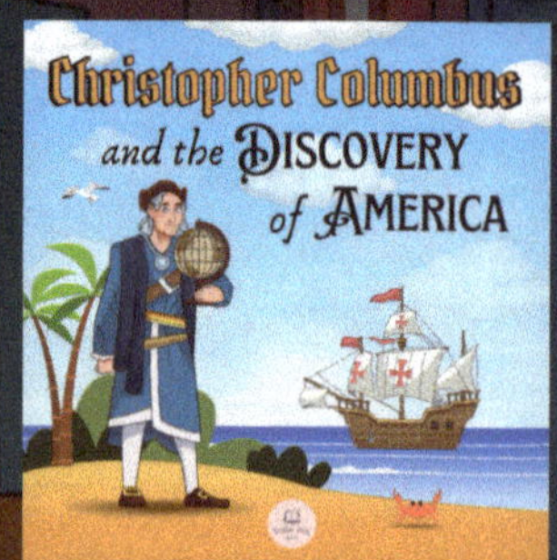

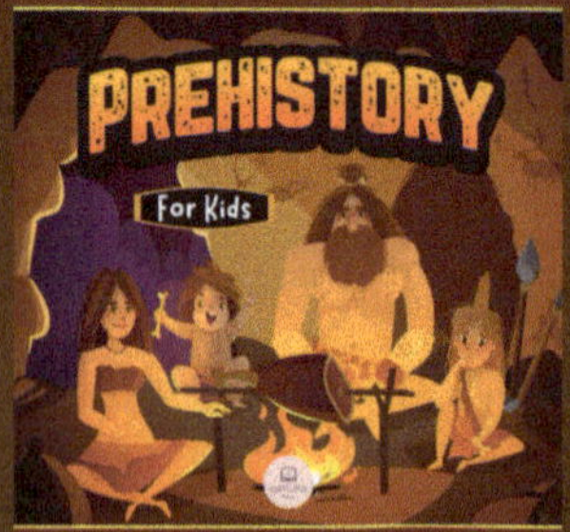

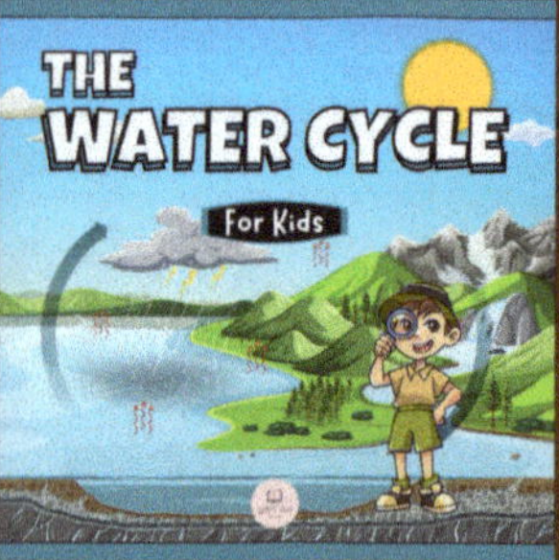

https://www.pge.me/childrensbooks

The Steadfast Tin Soldier
SCAN ME
www.azonlinks.com/841269984X
SAMMIE EXPLORES THE SOLAR SYSTEM
Ages 3-6
SCAN ME
www.azonlinks.com/8412699866

Subscribe to my newsletter, receive a free ebook, and stay informed of new publications, offers, and promotions of free books.

www.subscribepage.io/ebookfree

FOLLOW ME

www.amazon.com/author/samueljohnbooks

www.ingramcontent.com/pod-product-compliance
Lightning Source LLC
LaVergne TN
LVHW071005180726
843512LV00017B/1299